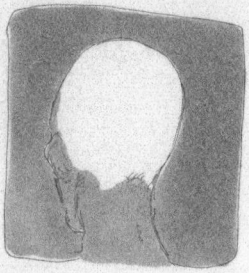

My editor, who had a perm, shaved his head. The following week a new editor was assigned to me: now I had two editors. The following week my new editor shaved his head. That same week I got a perm.

With the way things are going, I'm worried either Ichigo or I will end up with a shaved head due to some kind of accident.

–Tite Kubo

Bleach is author Tite Kubo's second title. Kubo made his debut with *ZOMBIEPOWDER.*, a four-volume series for *Weekly Shonen Jump*. To date, *Bleach* has been translated into numerous languages and has also inspired an animated TV series that began airing in the U.S. in 2006. Beginning its serialization in 2001, *Bleach* is still a mainstay in the pages of *Weekly Shonen Jump*. In 2005, *Bleach* was awarded the prestigious Shogakukan Manga Award in the *shonen* (boys) category.

D0028878

BLEACH
Vol. 42: SHOCK OF THE QUEEN
SHONEN JUMP Manga Edition

STORY AND ART BY
TITE KUBO

English Adaptation/Lance Caselman
Translation/Joe Yamazaki
Touch-up Art & Lettering/Mark McMurray
Design/Yukiko Whitley, Kam Li
Editor/Alexis Kirsch

BLEACH © 2001 by Tite Kubo. All rights reserved. First published in Japan in 2001 by SHUEISHA Inc., Tokyo. English translation rights arranged by SHUEISHA Inc.

The rights of the author(s) of the work(s) in this publication to be so identified have been asserted in accordance with Copyright, Designs and Patents Act 1988. A CIP catalogue record for this book is available from the British Library.

The stories, characters and incidents mentioned in this publication are entirely fictional.

No portion of this book may be reproduced or transmitted in any form or by any means without written permission from the copyright holders.

Printed in the U.S.A.

Published by VIZ Media, LLC
P.O. Box 77010
San Francisco, CA 94107

10 9 8 7 6 5 4 3 2 1
First printing, July 2012

www.viz.com

PARENTAL ADVISORY
BLEACH is rated T for Teen and is recommended for ages 13 and up. This volume contains fantasy violence.

ratings.viz.com

BLEACH ALL STORIES

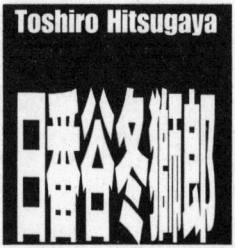

BLEACH 42

SHOCK OF THE QUEEN

Contents

359. The Frozen Obelisk	7
360. Shock of the Queen	27
361. I Hate Loneliness, But It Loves Me	47
362. Howling Wolves	67
363. Superchunky from Hell	87
364. Grinning Revengers	109
365. Whose Side Are We On	131
366. The Revenger's High	151
367. YOUR ENEMY IS MY ENEMY	171

STARS AND

スターク

Stark

Soi Fon

砕蜂

京楽春水

Shunsui Kyoraku

When high school student Ichigo Kurosaki meets Soul Reaper Rukia Kuchiki his life is changed forever. Soon Ichigo is a soul-cleansing Soul Reaper too, and he finds himself having adventures, as well as problems, that he never would have imagined. Now Ichigo and his friends must stop renegade Soul Reaper Aizen and his army of Arrancars from destroying the Soul Society and wiping out Karakura as well.

Though Ichigo defeats Ulquiorra and saves Orihime, the battle between the Thirteen Court Guard Companies and the Espadas in Karakura rages on! Despite their wounds, the captains each challenge a high-ranking Espada! Now it's Kyoraku vs. Stark, Soi Fon vs. Barragan, and Hitsugaya vs. Halibel! Who will win, and who will perish in these deadly duels?!

No world exists without sacrifice.
Do we not realize that we call
this hell where ash floats
upon a sea of blood, the world

BLEACH 42

SHOCK OF THE QUEEN

Shonen Jump Manga

Next Volume Preview

As the full extent of Barragan's power is revealed, the Soul Reapers and the Visoreds will have to team up to take him down. And when Aizen makes his first appearance on the battlefield, will things take a turn for the worse?

Coming July 2012!!

You're Reading in the Wrong Direction!!

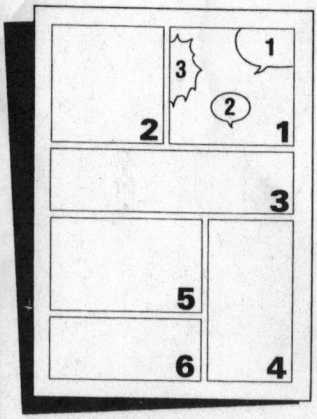

Whoops! Guess what? You're starting at the wrong end of the comic!

...It's true! In keeping with the original Japanese format, **Bleach** is meant to be read from right to left, starting in the upper-right corner.

Unlike English, which is read from left to right, Japanese is read from right to left, meaning that action, sound effects and word-balloon order are completely reversed... something which can make readers unfamiliar with Japanese feel pretty backwards themselves. For this reason, manga or Japanese comics published in the U.S. in English have sometimes been published "flopped"—that is, printed in exact reverse order, as though seen from the other side of a mirror.

By flopping pages, U.S. publishers can avoid confusing readers, but the compromise is not without its downside. For one thing, a character in a flopped manga series who once wore in the original Japanese version a T-shirt emblazoned with "M A Y" (as in "the merry month of") now wears one which reads "Y A M"! Additionally, many manga creators in Japan are themselves unhappy with the process, as some feel the mirror-imaging of their art skews their original intentions.

We are proud to bring you Tite Kubo's **Bleach** in the original unflopped format. For now, though, turn to the other side of the book and let the adventure begin...!

—Editor

CALGARY PUBLIC LIBRARY
JUL - 2012

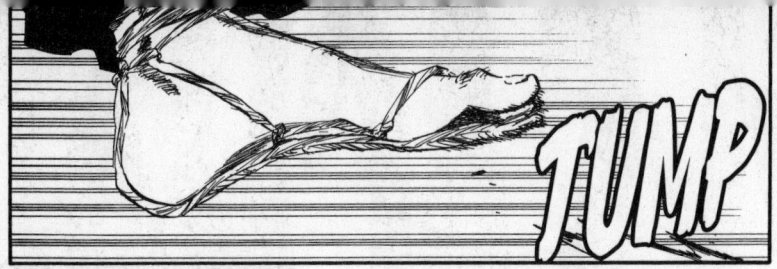

359. The Frozen Obelisk

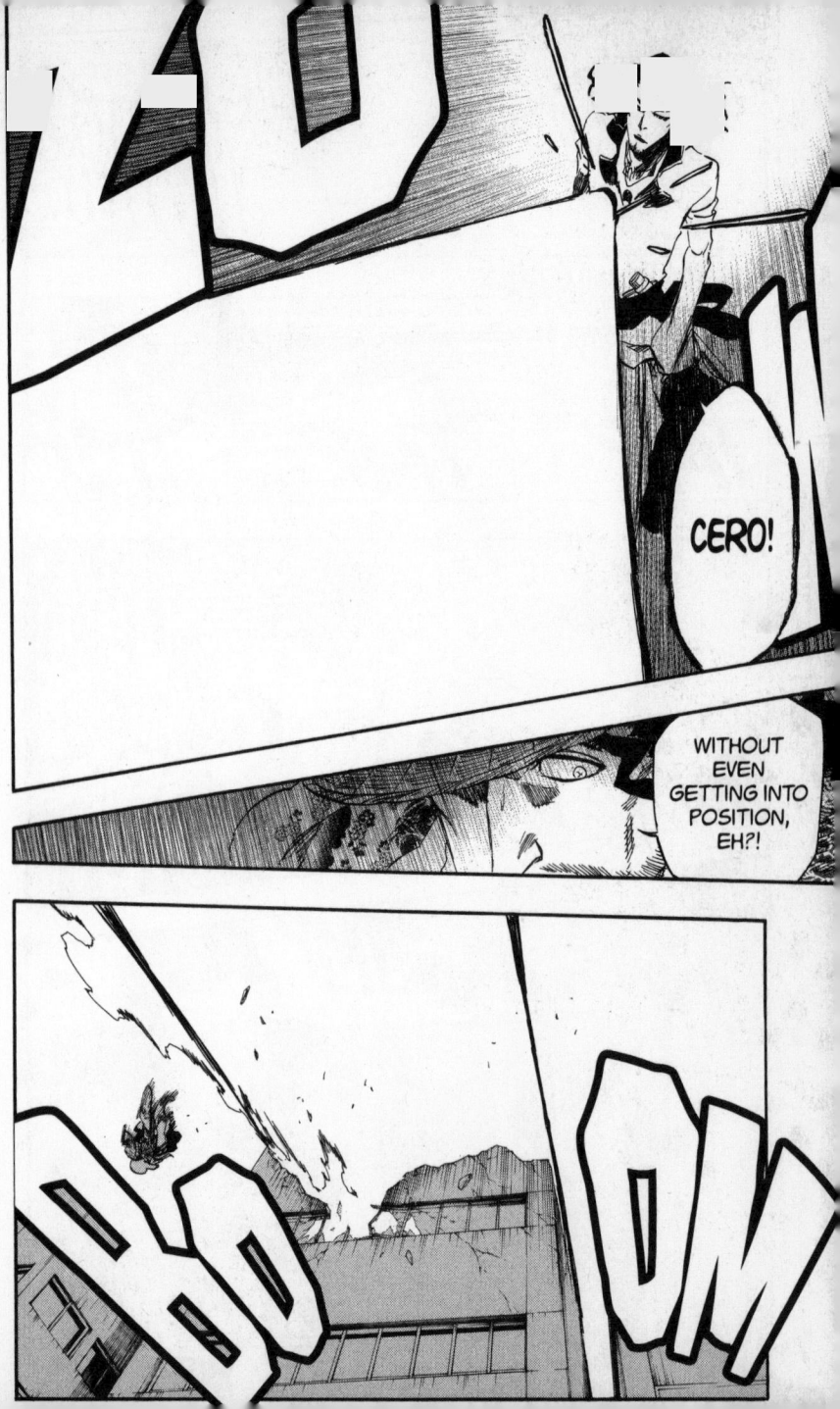
CERO!
WITHOUT EVEN GETTING INTO POSITION, EH?!
BOOM

STOP RUNNING AWAY.
WHAT'S HAPPENING ?!
WHAT THE HELL IS THIS?
PRMM

BLEACH
359. The Frozen Obelisk
WHAT ...
IS THIS ...!?

TENSÔ JÛRIN.
(WEATHER SUBJUGATION)
ONE OF HYÔRINMARU'S BASIC ABILITIES...
...WHICH ALSO HAPPENS TO BE ITS GREATEST ABILITY.

MY POWERS ARE STILL UNRE-FINED.
I KNOW THAT BETTER THAN ANYONE.
THAT'S WHY I DIDN'T WANT TO USE THIS ABILITY IN ITS BANKAI STATE.
CAN'T SEE US ANYMORE, KEEP GOING.

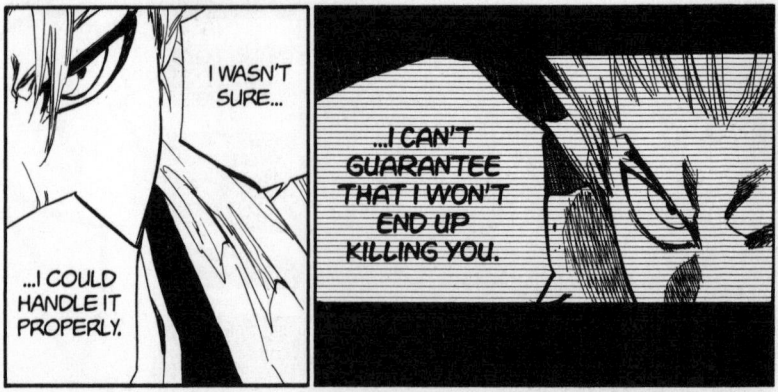
I WASN'T SURE...
...I COULD HANDLE IT PROPERLY.
...I CAN'T GUARANTEE THAT I WON'T END UP KILLING YOU.

READ THIS WAY
...IT LOOKS LIKE MY CONCERNS WERE UN-FOUNDED.
BUT NOW THAT HALF THE ICE FLOWERS BEHIND ME HAVE FALLEN...
ESPADA TRES.
TIER HALIBEL.
I WILL ...
...ASK YOU YOUR NAME, ESPADA.
ARE YOU READY?
CAPTAIN OF TENTH COMPANY.
I'M TÔSHIRÔ HITSUGAYA ...

HYÔTEN HAKKASÔ.
(FROZEN HEAVENS HUNDRED FLOWER FUNERAL)

!
KSH
CHANK
HIRVI—
KSHHHH
FWUP

WHAT THE...
POOF
POOF
POOF
POOF
POOF

HYÔTEN HAKKASÔ.
ANYTHING THAT SNOW TOUCHES...
...INSTANTLY FREEZES INTO THE SHAPE OF A FLOWER.
WHAT IS THIS ?!
BY THE TIME A HUNDRED FLOWERS HAVE BLOSSOMED...

...YOUR LIFE WILL HAVE DIS-APPEARED.

I COULDN'T LET YOU AVENGE YOUR SUBORDINATES' DEATHS.
SORRY.

RUMMMMMMMMM

RRMMM
IS THAT CAPTAIN HITSU-GAYA'S ATTACK ?!
WHAT IS THAT?!
ICE ?!
W–
RRMMMMMM

WHAP
WHOA !!
W–
SHR

NO!!
HMPH.
WOO O
FWUFF
RESPIRA.

WOOS
WOOS
Woo
IT'S THAT THING!! IT'S COMING TOWARD ME!!
WAH!!

Shlu p
Stik
WOOOOOOO?!
WHAT'S WRONG?
CAN'T YOU EVEN EVADE THAT ONE? I DISCHARGED THAT RESPIRA SLOWLY ON PURPOSE.
HOW...
...COMICAL.
HWA HA HA HA HA HA HA HA HA HA HA HA HA!!
IMPOS-SIBLE.
I CAN'T FIGHT THIS!
I'LL GET KILLED...
...FOR REAL!!

C—
CAPTAIN !!
RRMMMMMMM
HFF
HFF
CRYING OUT LIKE A COWARD ...
FOOL.
SAVE ME!!
...I'LL BEAT HIM EVEN UGLIER THAN HE IS.
WHEN THIS FIGHT IS OVER..
THAT SHOULD BE ENOUGH.
ALL RIGHT.

BA-
AM
BAN...
...KAI!
WMM

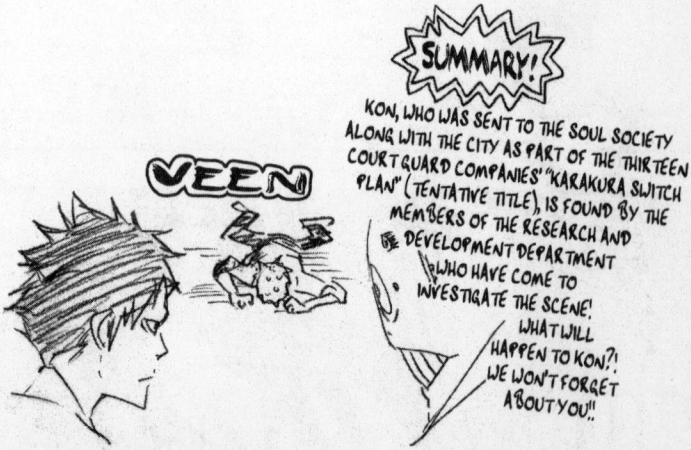
SUMMARY!
KON, WHO WAS SENT TO THE SOUL SOCIETY ALONG WITH THE CITY AS PART OF THE THIRTEEN COURT GUARD COMPANIES' "KARAKURA SWITCH PLAN" (TENTATIVE TITLE), IS FOUND BY THE MEMBERS OF THE RESEARCH AND DEVELOPMENT DEPARTMENT WHO HAVE COME TO INVESTIGATE THE SCENE!
WHAT WILL HAPPEN TO KON?! WE WON'T FORGET ABOUT YOU!!
VEEN

RAAAAA!!
360. Shock of the Queen
ALL RIGHT, C'MON !!
WHUP
KRSHH
SPRSHH

W—
WAAAAAAH!!
KEEP IT COMING !!
SHRSH
THUMP
THUD
UGH...
UH...

WAAAAAAH!
I'LL KILL YOU !!
THAT'S THE SPIRIT !!

TMP TMP TMP TMP TMP TMP TMP
GIMME BACK MY SWORD !!
I CAN'T DO THAT!!

SWUP
THUD
WAAH !!
PUT MORE OOMPH INTO IT!
DIE, YOU GRAY-HAIRED GEEZER!!

Bleach 360. Shock of the Queen

TMP TMP TMP
W—
WAAAAAAH!!
TMP TMP TMP TMP TMP

TMP
YOOH
TUMP

YOU'RE JUST JEALOUS BECAUSE YOU'RE A SKELETON !!
SH—
SHUT UP!!
CHAK

...FOR A CHUNK OF MEAT.
YOU'RE GOOD AT RUNNING AWAY...

CRUSH...
...GEGE-TSUBURI !!
KRRR
UD

WHAK
WHAK
WHAK
WHAKWHAK
VWMM

THEY DISINTE-GRATED!
IT DIDN'T WORK!!
CRAP !!
TMP

ARGH!! WHY ISN'T MY ZANPAKU-TÔ A KIDÔ-TYPE THAT CAN SHOOT FLAME OR ICE?!
TMP TMP TMP TMP
!

THAT'S IT! A KIDÔ!!
A KIDÔ WILL GET TO HIM!!
I'VE DISCOVER-ED YOUR WEAKNESS !!

BO
OM
SWAK
B–
BAKUDÔ 2!!!
SEKIENTON!! (RED SMOKE ESCAPE)

WOOOOOOO
WUFF WUFF WUFF WUFF

C–
COME TO THINK OF IT, I CAN BARELY USE KIDÔ.
PHEW, THAT WAS CLOSE. I ALMOST MADE HIM MAD.
WASH

...THAT'S ABOUT ALL HE CAN DO.
LOOKS LIKE...
HMPH.

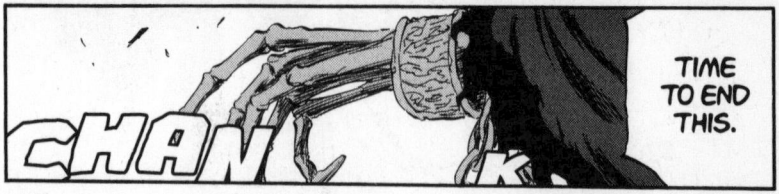
TIME TO END THIS.
CHAN

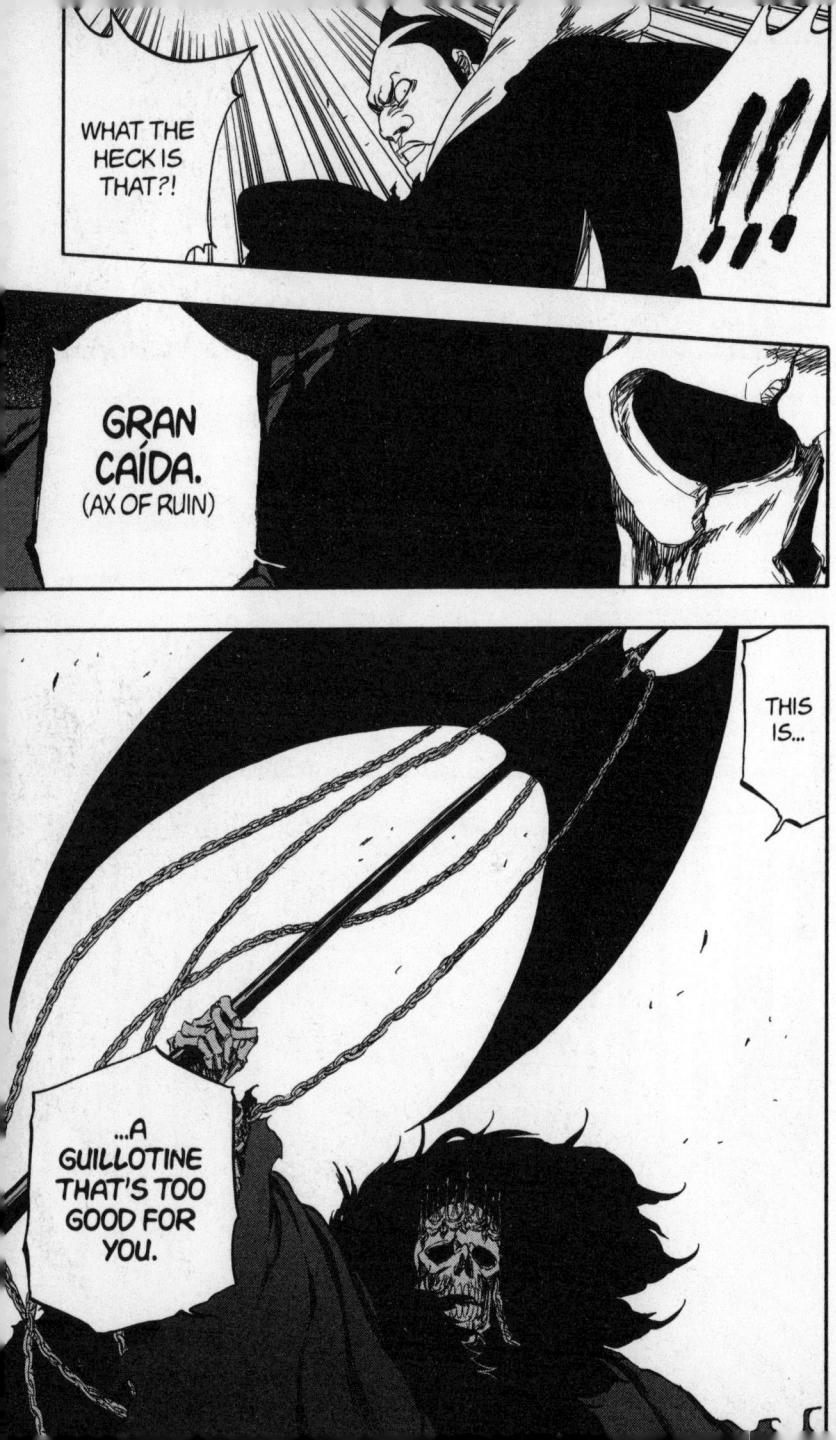
WHAT THE HECK IS THAT?!
!!!
GRAN CAÍDA.
(AX OF RUIN)
THIS IS...
...A GUILLOTINE THAT'S TOO GOOD FOR YOU.

DECAY AND...
...DIE.
EEP...
BAN...
...KAI!!
THO
OM

KLANG
KLANG
KL ANG
KL ANG

JAKUHÔ RAIKÔBEN.
(HORNET THUNDER WHIP)

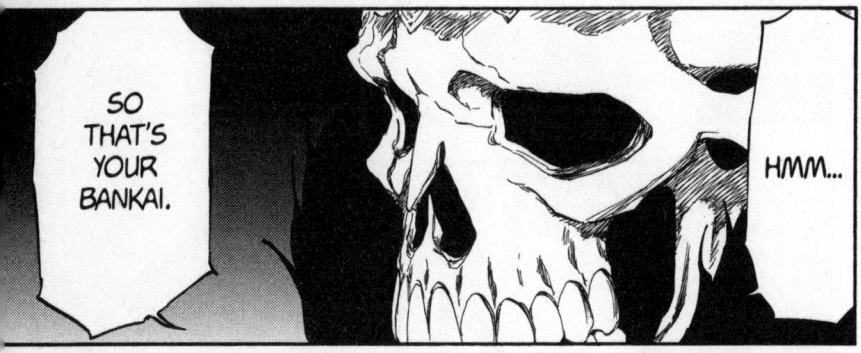
HMM...
SO THAT'S YOUR BANKAI.

WHAT IS THAT SHAPE?
HOW'S SHE GOING TO FIGHT WITH THAT?

SO THAT'S CAPTAIN SOI FON'S BANKAI!
IT'S MY FIRST TIME SEEING IT.

C–
CAP-TAIN !!

A STEEL BAND USED AS AN UNDER-LAYER FOR ARMOR!
THAT'S A GINJÔTAN!

WITH THAT THING WRAPPED AROUND HER, EVEN CAPTAIN SOI FON'S MOVEMENTS WILL BE HINDERED.
WHY DID SHE WRAP HERSELF IN SOME-THING SO HEAVY?

WHAT ?
...WITH-OUT USING THIS BANKAI.
...TO END THIS...
I HOPED ...

THIS BANKAI VIOLATES MY SECRET POLICE STANDARDS.
SHANK
AND ITS ATTACK...
IT'S TOO BIG TO CONCEAL ...
TOO HEAVY TO MOVE ABLY...
...AN ASSASSIN.
...IS TOO FLASHY FOR...
MMMM

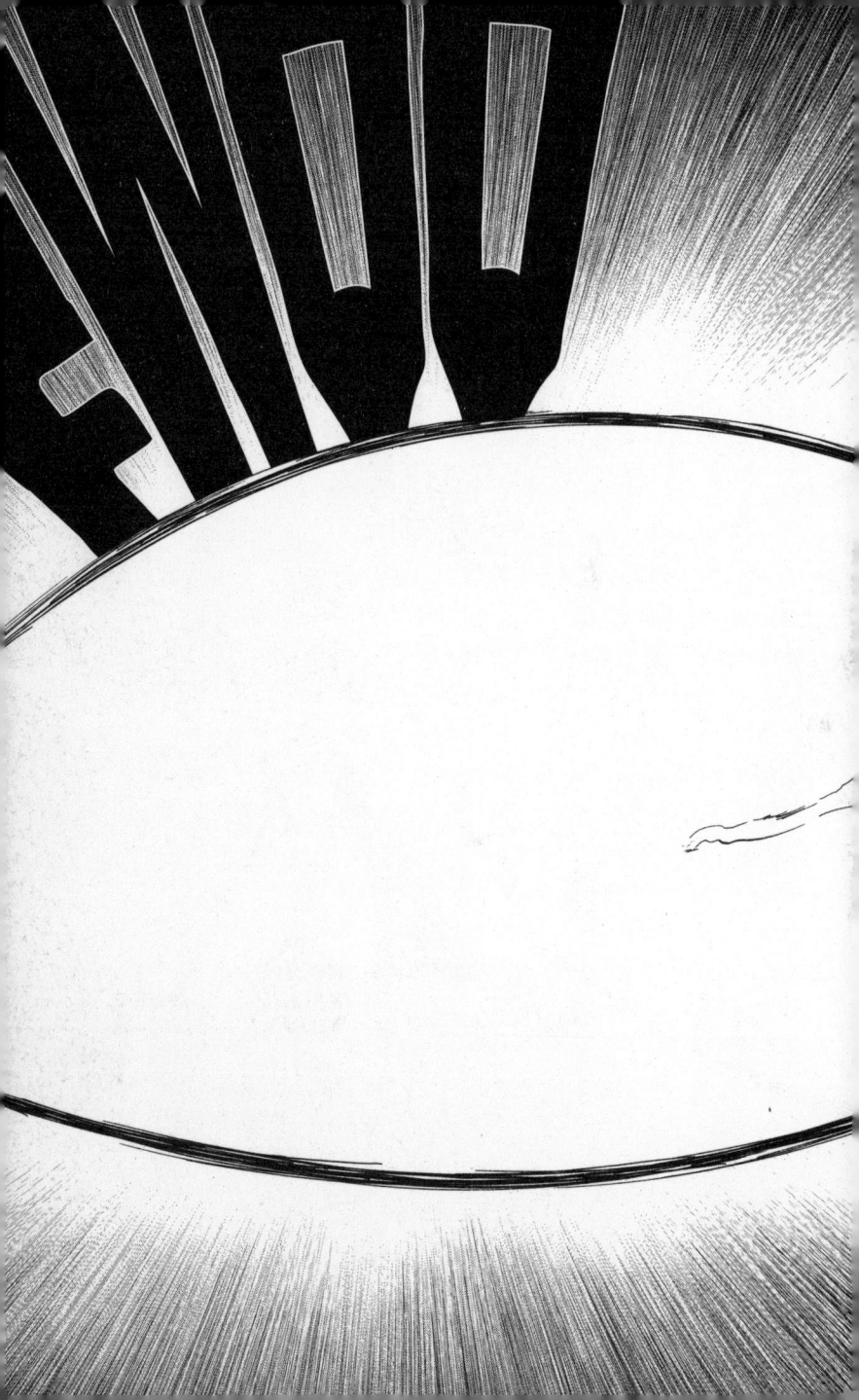
FIGU

WHOA!
YOU'RE TOO CLOSE, TOO CLOSE, TOO CLOSE!
I CAN'T SEE, BUT I BET HE'S LOOKING AT ME
FROM REAL CLOSE!! STOP LOOKING AT ME!
GO AWAY! GIMME A BREAK!!
GO AWAY.
JUST GO AWAY.
DON'T COME NEAR ME.
STOP LOOKING AT ME.
VEEN

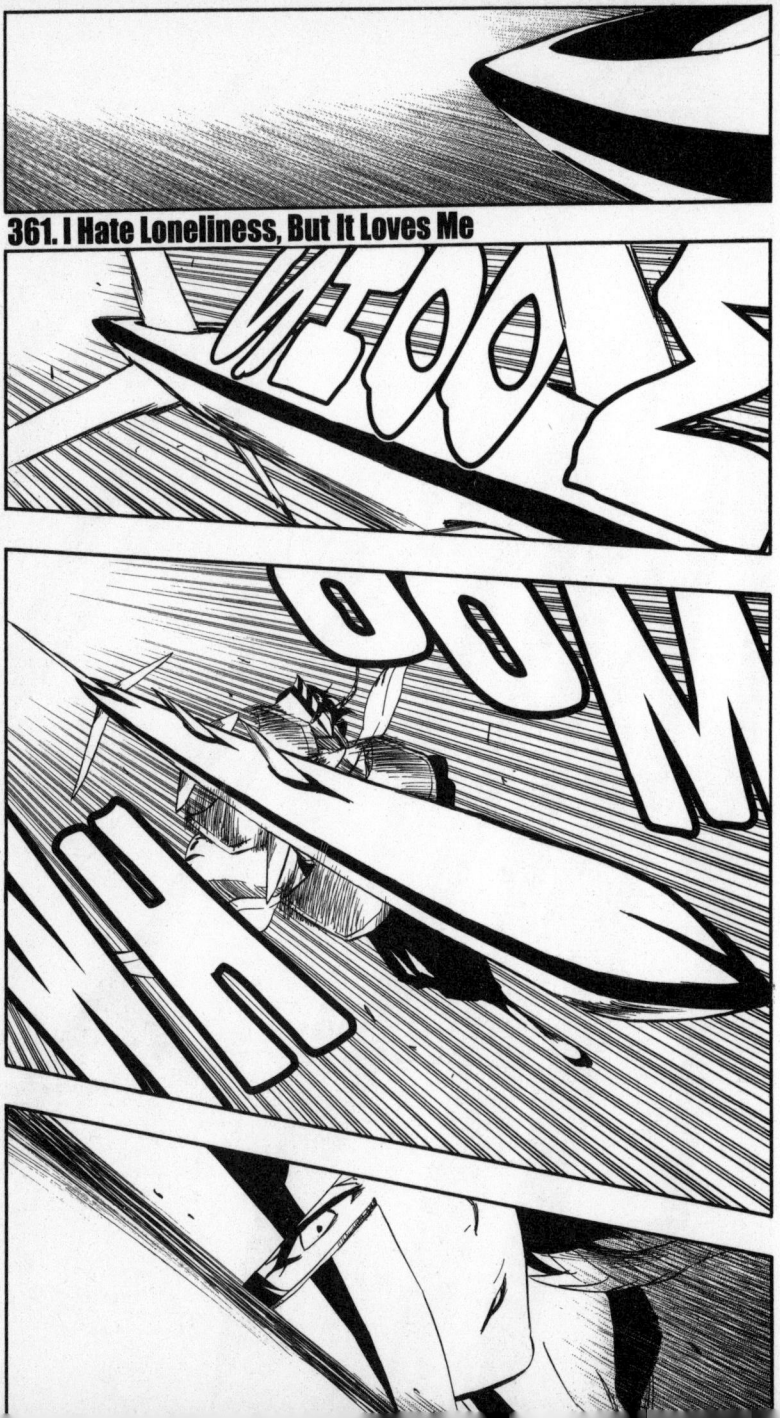

361. I Hate Loneliness, But It Loves Me

DOOM

WHAM
UGH...
AAAAAAH!!
KRUNCH
CH
KRUNCH
KRUNCH
UNH ...
DAMN ...

WHAP
DID...
DID I...
...GET HIM?
WHUP
SNAP
SHRRRK

WHAM
KLAK KLAK
CAPTAIN...

TAKE YOUR HANDS OFF ME.

DISGUSTING.

361.

I Hate Loneliness, But It Loves Me

BLEACH

WOOOOOOOO

HEY.

I THINK SO.
BANKAI IS OUR ACE IN THE HOLE.
SO THEY GOTTA BE PRETTY IM-PRESSIVE!

ARE ALL YOUR BANKAIS ...
...THAT POWERFUL?

BETWEEN THE BANKAI OF THAT ICE GUY OVER THERE AND YOURS...
...WHICH IS STRONGER?

SO...

RIGHT NOW YOU'RE STILL STRONGER THAN HIM.

UKITAKE !!
FWAP
KYO-RAKU ...
HOLD ON TO THAT.
FWUP
WA...
WHOA!
FWUP

THIS GUY...
...IS FINALLY READY TO GO AT IT.

YEAH.

I WANT TO SEE...

...WHAT YOUR BANKAI ARE LIKE.

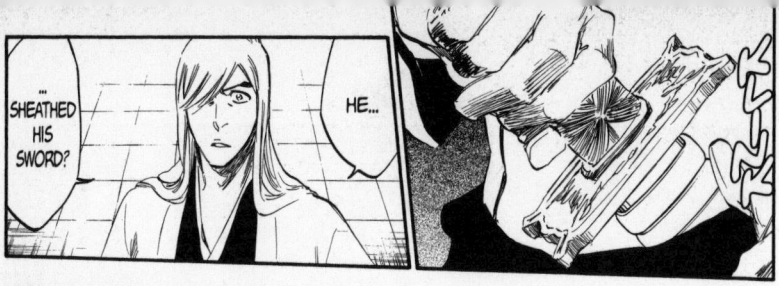
...SHEATHED HIS SWORD?
HE...

TW!
TCH
LILI-NETTE !!

GET OVER HERE.

...?
WHY DO YOU NEED HER?
DON'T SHOUT! YOU SCARED ME!
D-
TUMP

THE TWO OF US MAKE ONE.

THE HOLLOW POWERS ...
...THAT OTHER ARRANCARS DIVIDE BETWEEN THEIR BODIES AND SWORDS...
...WE SPLIT BETWEEN TWO BODIES.

WHEN WE BECOME ONE...
...OUR POWER IS RELEASED.
WM M

GIVE CHASE ...
...LOS LOBOS.
(WOLVES)

KRM
KATEN KYÔKOTSU. (FLOWER-HEAVEN BONE OF MADNESS)
WOOOO

WHAT THE HECK IS THIS?! IS IT NECESSARY TO LOOK AT ME SO CLOSE UP?! WHAT IS THIS?! WHAT'S GOING ON?!
KLIK KLIK KLIK KLIK KLIK KLIK KLIK
AAAAAAAAH!!

WOOSH
362. Howling Wolves
WOOOOOL
WOOOOO

FWOO...
ALL RIGHT...
...THEN...
CHAK

...GET GOING...
OKAY...
SHALL WE...
CHAK
...LILI-NETTE ?
...
WHAK
OW!!
DON'T IGNORE ME!

BLEACH 362. Howling Wolves

THAT HURT!! YOU COULD'VE CRACKED MY HEAD OPEN! STARK, YOU FOOL!!

HOW AM I SUPPOSED TO KNOW WHERE YOUR HEAD IS ANY-WAY?!
IT'S YOUR OWN FAULT FOR NOT COOPER-ATING!
SHUT UP!

OW! OW! OW! THAT'S MY BUTT!!
HOW MANY TIMES DO I HAVE TO TELL YOU?! THE TIP IS MY HEAD...
SKRIK SKRI
YOU KNOW EXACTLY WHAT YOU'RE DOING!!
OW!!

YAA!

THAT'S JUST–
ATTACKING ME IN THE MIDDLE OF A CONVERSATION, EH?
BUSHÔ GOMA!! (WOBBLY TOP)
WOOSH

OOM!
TAKA ONI.
(MOUNTAIN DEMON)

AK
TU
MP
LET ME FINISH WHAT I WAS SAYING.
YOUR SURPRISE ATTACK BETRAYS A LACK OF CONFI-DENCE.
THAT'S NOT LIKE YOU.
WELL ...
I WAS HOPING TO KILL YOU WITH MY FIRST STRIKE.
BUT YOU EVADED IT. YOUR RELEASED STATE IS IMPRES-SIVE.
AT ANY RATE...

THAT'S RIGHT.
...
THAT GUN IN YOUR HAND...
...CAN FIRE CERO BLASTS.

IT CAN'T.
...FIRE SOME-THING ELSE TOO?
COULD IT MAY-BE...

THAT WOULD BE MY QUES-TION.
WHAT'S THE POINT OF HIDING IT?
YOU'RE A BAD LIAR.

CHAK
YOU'RE GOING TO SHOW ME YOUR BANKAI EVEN IF I HAVE TO MAKE YOU.
I WENT TO THE TROUBLE OF RE-LEASING.
YOU MAY HAVE GOTTEN STRONGER BY RE-LEASING ...
NO, NO.
...BUT ORDINARY CERO WON'T...
VW
MM
SHUDDER

BAM
BAM
CERO METRAL-LETA (SUBMACHINE GUN)

BAM
BAM
BAM
BAM
BAM

WM
BAM
BAM
BAM
BAM
BAM
BAM
BAM
BAM
BAM
BAM
BAM
BA

IT'S USELESS TO RUN AWAY.
BAM BAM BAM BAM
BAM BAM BAM
ISN'T THIS A LITTLE UNFAIR?!
W–
WAIT A SECOND !!
BAM BAM BAM BAM

SOGYÔ NO KOTOWARI.
(LAW OF THE TWIN FISH)
DO
ON

SWO
WHAT THE ?!
WAS THAT A...
...CERO?!

HUH? SOMEBODY'S HERE. NOT SO FAST. NO ORDINARY GIRL CAN GET ME TO COME OUT OF MY PRETEND SLEEP.
HEY, YOU...
TMP
WHAT'S GOING ON? WHAT'RE THEY WHISPERING ABOUT? THAT "KLAKKA, KLAKKA" SOUND WAS COMING FROM YOUR HEAD?!
KLAKKA KLAKKA
WSP WSP WSP
HUH? THEY'RE SUDDENLY BACKING AWAY?

BLEACH
ブリーチ

BLEACH
ブリーチ

WHAT...
...WAS THAT?

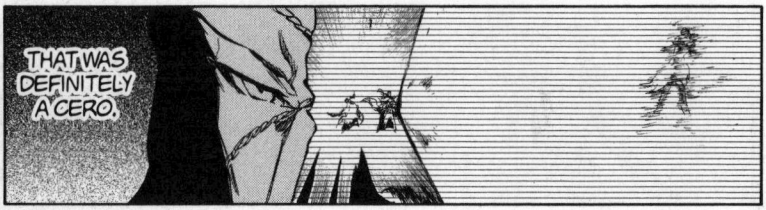
THAT WAS DEFINITELY A CERO.

DOO OOM

WE'RE BASICALLY UP AGAINST TWO OF THEM.
I DON'T WANT TO HEAR IT.
IT'S NOT COWARDLY FOR ME TO ASSIST YOU.
UKI-TAKE...

NO.
DON'T.
NO, NO.
I WAS GOING TO.
BESIDES, IT DOESN'T SEEM LIKE YOU'RE WILLING TO USE YOUR BANKAI.

YOUR BANKAI...
...SHOULDN'T BE DONE WHERE EVERYBODY CAN SEE IT.

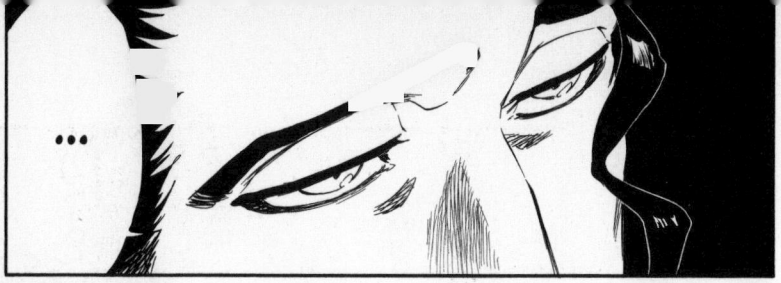
...

HEY, YOU...
...MY ABILITY IS MORE EFFECTIVE.
BESIDES, AGAINST AN ENEMY LIKE THIS...

HOW DID YOU FIRE A CERO JUST NOW?
NO, NOT YOU.
I'M TALKING TO THE WHITE-HAIRED CAPTAIN.

I SEE.
MAYBE I'LL KNOW IF YOU SHOOT ME AGAIN!
I DON'T KNOW.
HOW DID I?

CHK
I THINK YOU'RE RIGHT.

STARK!
HEY!

YOU KNOW WHAT'S GOING ON, RIGHT?
IT'S A TRAP, STARK.
YOU DO, DON'T YOU?

SHUT UP.

BLEACH

BLOW
DOWN

363.

Superchunky from Hell

ARE YOU LISTENING TO ME, STARK?!
WHAT DID I TELL YOU?!
HE FIRED IT BACK!
SEE?!
THAK
BOOM

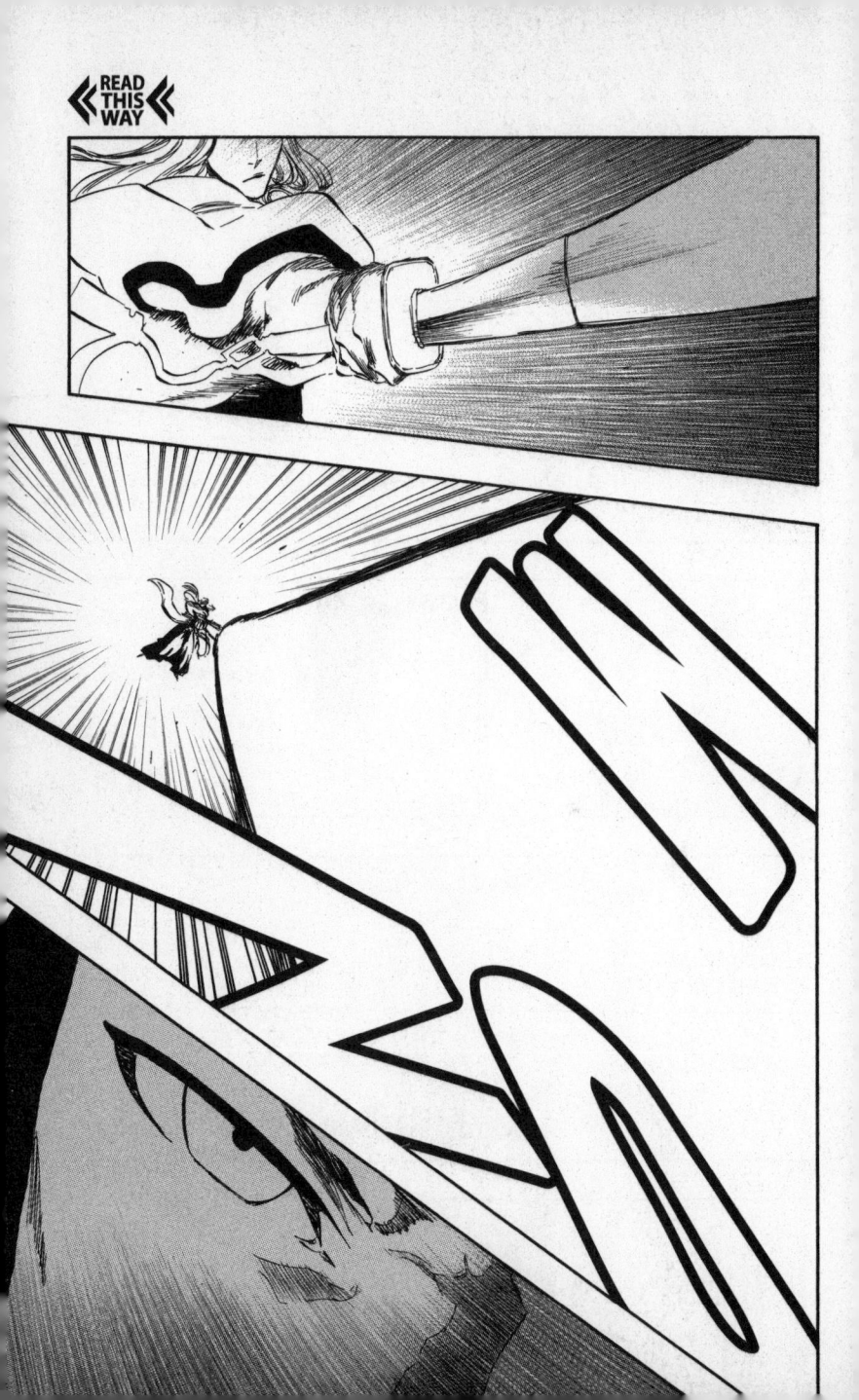
READ THIS WAY

AND THAT'S NOT ALL.

I SEE.
YOU CAN AB-SORB...
...AN ENEMY'S ATTACK AND FIRE IT RIGHT BACK AT HIM.

THE FIVE TALISMANS HANGING FROM YOUR ROPE...
...ADJUST THE VELOCITY AND PRESSURE OF THE REDIRECTED ATTACK...
...THROWING OFF THE ENEMY'S ABILITY TO EVADE IT.

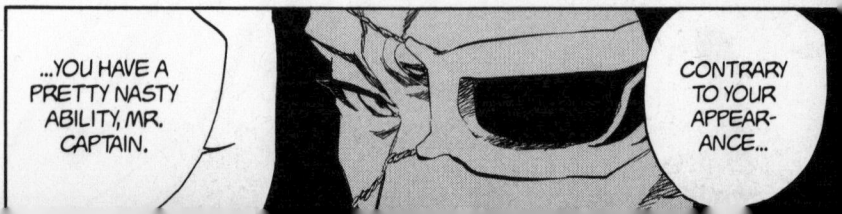
CONTRARY TO YOUR APPEAR-ANCE...
...YOU HAVE A PRETTY NASTY ABILITY, MR. CAPTAIN.

I'M IM-PRESSED!
I DIDN'T THINK YOU'D FIGURE IT OUT IN ONLY THREE ATTACKS!
THANKS.
BUT I'M GLAD...
...YOUR ABILITY ISN'T SOME MINDLESS ONE THAT ONLY REFLECTS YOUR ENEMY'S ATTACK BACK AT HIM.
IF THE ATTACK HAS TO BE AB-SORBED ...
...THERE MUST BE A LIMIT TO HOW MUCH IT CAN ABSORB.
IF I FIRE A THOUSAND ROUNDS...
...AT ONE SPOT IN AN INSTANT, YOU SHOULDN'T BE ABLE TO FIRE THEM ALL BACK.
CHAK

SWUP
DOSH

KA-
BLAM!
I'LL TELL YOU SOMETHING ABOUT MYSELF.
I ACT HOWEVER I FEEL LIKE.
IT'S NOT GOOD TO TELL ME WHO I AM, MR. ESPADA.
I TOLD YOU NOT TO DO SOMETHING THAT'S NOT LIKE YOU, MR. CAPTAIN!
...YOU AND I WERE ALIKE.
HMPH.
AND HERE I WAS THINK-ING...

SNAP
KREEK

...THESE THREE ESPADA LEADERS.
I HATE TO THINK THERE ARE OTHERS HERE TO HELP...

A NEW ENEMY COMING ?!
GAR-GANTA !

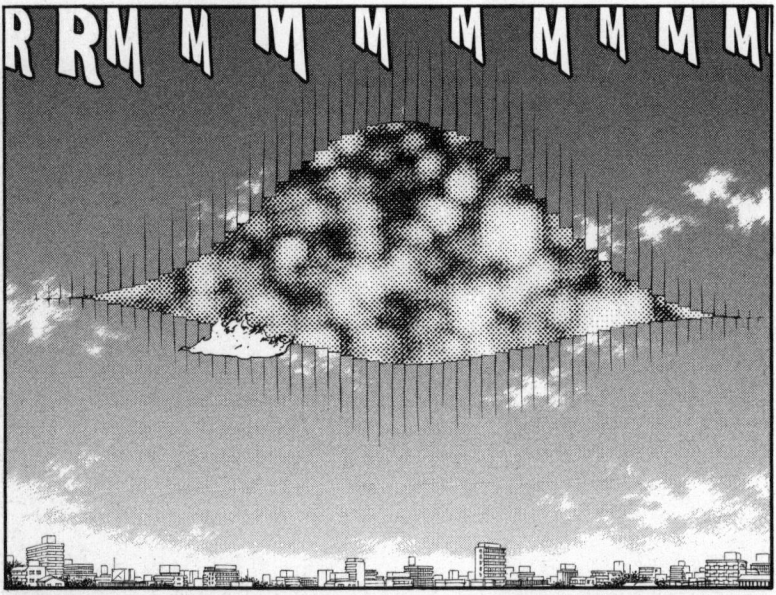
RRMMMMMMMMM

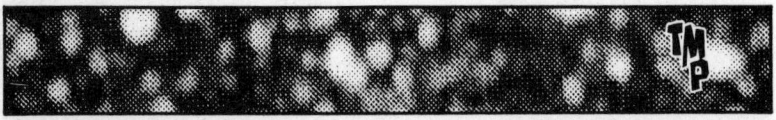
TMP

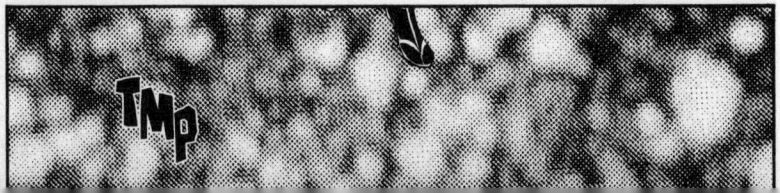
TMP

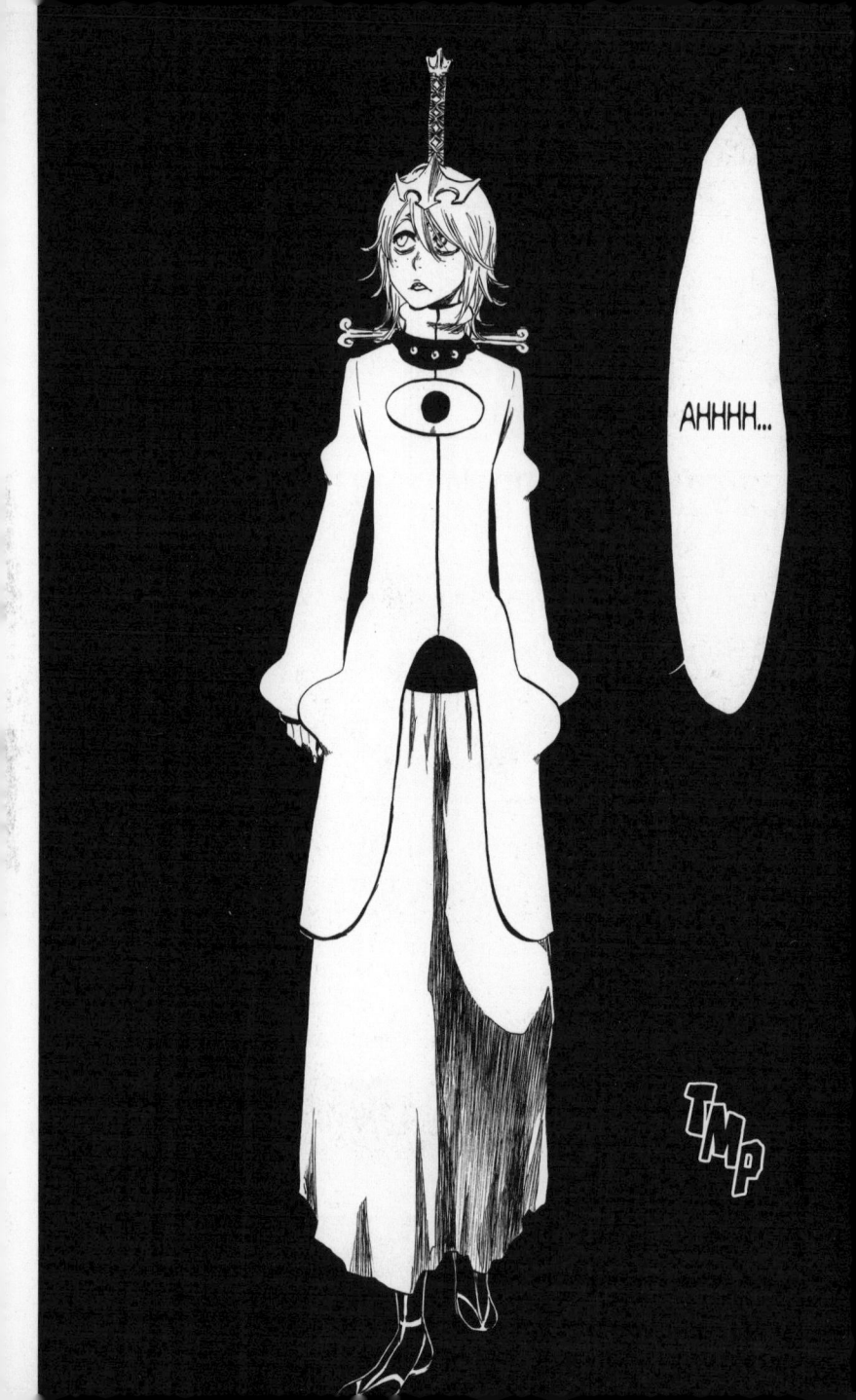
AHHHH...
TMP

SOMETHING STRANGE JUST SHOWED UP.
...
...IS THAT ?
WHO...
WONDER-WEISS...
AWW...
TUMB

NO!

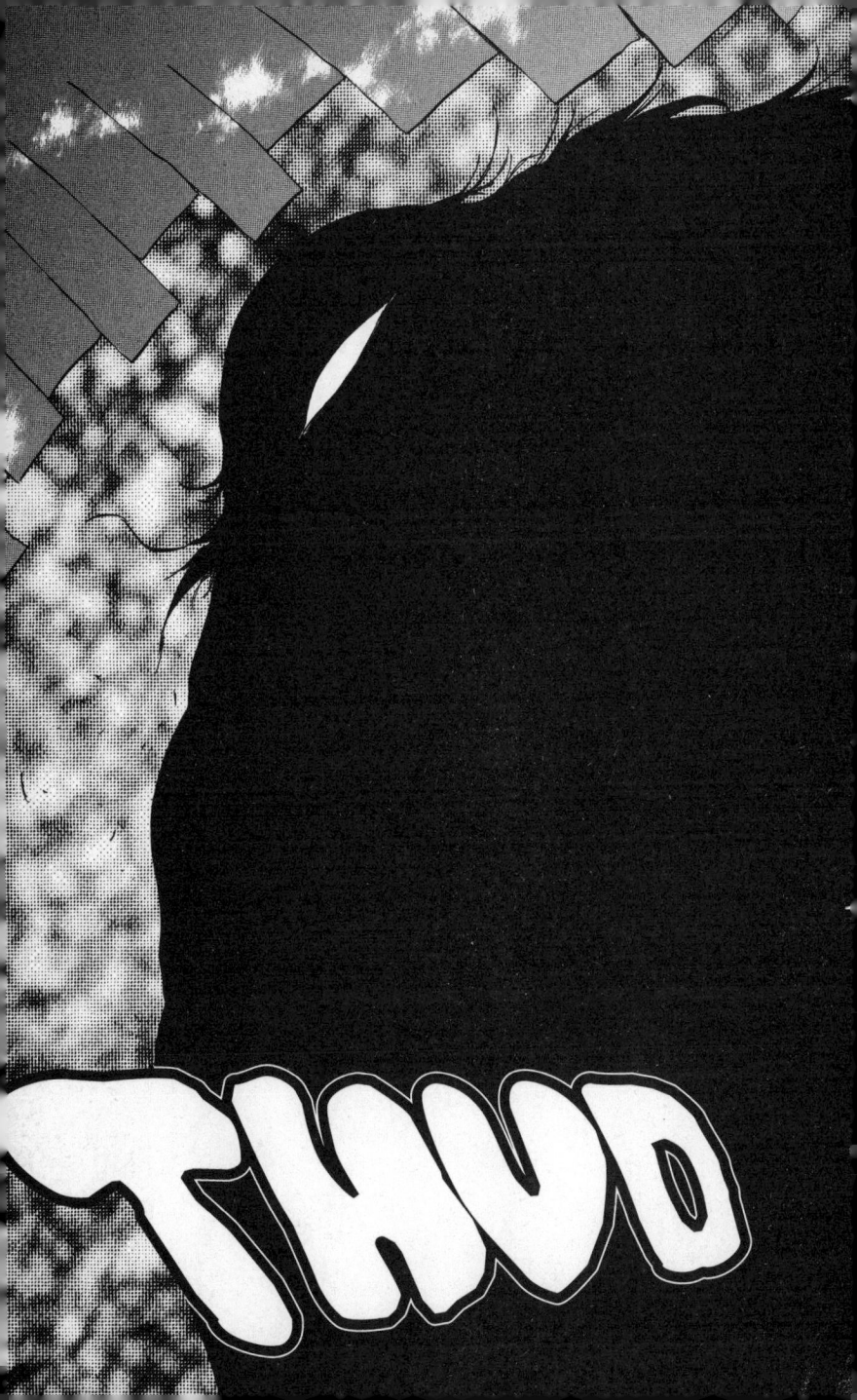
THUD

DO
OM
WE'RE FROM THE RE-SEARCH AND DEVELOPMENT DEPARTMENT. WE DO ANGELIC WORK.
DO
OM
WAKE UP.
DOOM
WE'RE HERE TO HELP YOU.
YOU'LL CATCH A COLD SLEEPING THERE.
NOW WAKE UP.

BLEACH
ブリーチ

BLEACH
ブリーチ

SWUP

BLEACH 364. Grinning Revengers

READ THIS WAY
FROM THAT TIME?!
THAT EYE...
TUMP
AHHH...

SHUNK

WHUP
WHA-

AWWWWW...
SNUP

TAT
BO
SORRY.

IF WONDER-WEISS IS HERE THAT CAN ONLY MEAN...
...THAT LORD AIZEN'S PATIENCE HAS BEEN EXHAUSTED.
SHUNSUI!
JUSHIRO!!
HAA...

KRAK

KRAK KRAK KRAK KRAK
!
KREESH

FW OOF
CAPTAIN KOMA-MURA!!
...CAN'T BE...
IT...

KIRA ...

YOU'VE DONE MORE THAN ENOUGH HERE.
PLEASE GO...

PLEASE GO!!

CAPTAIN KOMA-MURA !!!
PLEASE GO!!

...OUR SURVIVAL MEANS NOTHING!!
YOU COULD KEEP PROTECT-ING US HERE...
...BUT IF EVERY-BODY ELSE GETS KILLED...

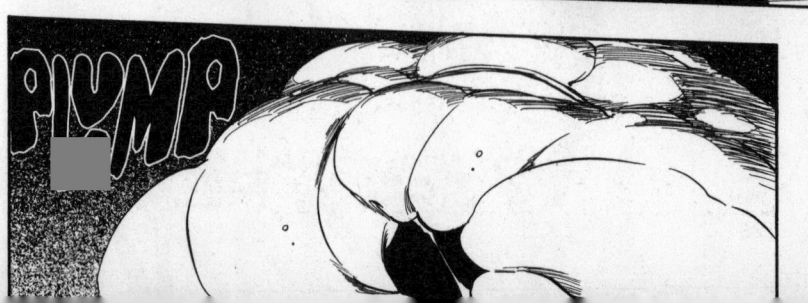
PUMP

FWOOOSH
WHAT A STENCH...
AS USUAL.
I AGREE.
THIS IS WHAT THEY MEAN...
...WHEN THEY TALK ABOUT THE SMELL OF DEATH.
IT'S ALL RIGHT.
THE SMELL OF DEATH...
RMMMM!

...IS PERFECTLY APPROPRIATE HERE.

AAH...
AH...

THIS IS REALLY ...
...THE END !!
TMP

NOT SO FAST.
...AIZEN.
IT'S BEEN A WHILE...

WH
UNKNOWN BOOB LADY!!
AWAKE!
I...
...AM...
UP
SHEEEEEEEEEN

365. Whose Side Are We On

IT'S BEEN A WHILE...

BLEACH365: Whose Side Are We On

THAT'S...

WHAT THE... THEY'RE...

SHINJI HIRAKO!

SO YOU WERE...
...HIDING IN THE WORLD OF THE LIVING.

HUFF
HUFF

...

IT'S BEEN A LONG TIME.
ANYBODY YOU WANNA SAY HI TO IN THE THIRTEEN COURT GUARD COMPANIES?
NOT ME!

SHUT UP, HIYORI!
I WASN'T ASKING YOU!
WHAT DO YOU MEAN?!
YOU WERE ASKING EVERY-BODY!
I DON'T REALLY NEED TO.
I'M OKAY TOO.

NO-BODY ...
...IN THE THIR-TEEN COURT GUARD COMPA-NIES.
ME NEITHER!
STRAW-BERRY'S NOT HERE?
WHY?
...

HEY!
POOF
WHERE ARE YOU GOING, LISA!!
WELL, I SHOULD ...
...GO SAY HELLO TO THE CAPTAIN GENERAL.

HEY!
WAIT, SHINJI !!

KLINK

TUNK
HOW LONG ARE YOU GONNA PLAY DEAD?!
UGH!
OUCH.
KLAK
WELL...

I'LL BE...
I HAVEN'T SEEN YOU FOR A WHILE AND NOW LOOK AT YOU. YOU'RE BEAUTIFUL.

THWAK
OOF!!

I'M GLAD TO SEE YOU'RE ALL RIGHT.

TMP
STAY THERE!
I'LL SHOW YOU HOW STRONG I'VE BECOME!
LISA ...

IDIOT!

SSH

I COULDN'T AGREE MORE.

HAVE YOU COME ...
...SEEKING REVENGE?

IF I HATE YOU FOR ANY-THING...
...IT'S FOR FIGHTING INSIDE A SUPER-STRONG FORCE FIELD!

YEAH, AGAINST AIZEN.
I DON'T REALLY CARE ABOUT YOU.

I AM SORRY, SIR!
I WASN'T SURE I SHOULD LET THEM IN, BUT AFTER SEEING THE SITUATION INSIDE...
IT'S FINE.
IF WE DIDN'T FIND THIS GUY PATROLLING THE OUTSIDE, WE WOULD'VE BEEN GOING AROUND IN CIRCLES FOREVER!
ZSH

SHINJI HIRAKO...

CAN WE...
...CON-SIDER YOU...
...OUR ALLIES FOR NOW?

WHAT DO YOU THINK?

OF COURSE NOT.

KLIK

AND...

WE'RE AIZEN'S ENEMIES.

WE'RE NOT YOUR ALLIES.

...ICHIGO'S ALLY.
ICHI-GO...
...KURO-SAKI?
WM
M
NO, BUT I THINK WE'RE OUT OF TIME.
ARE YOU DONE TALKING TO HIM?
YOU'RE FINALLY BACK.
WM
M

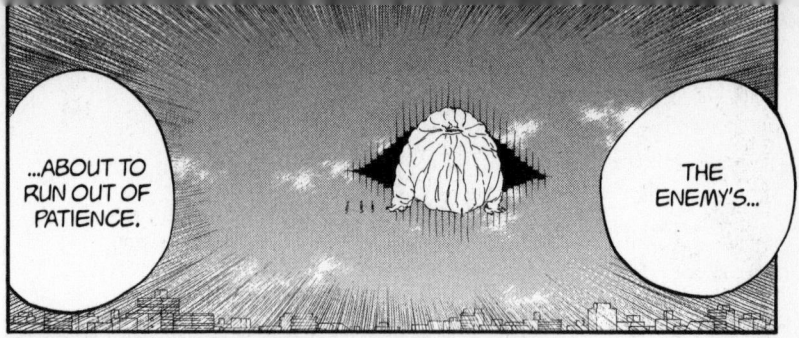

UHHH....
AHHH....
AAAA

SHUT UP AND WATCH.
WHAT'S IT DOING?!

SPLOOSH
WHAT THE...

GLOOP
SHLUK
GLUP

ARE THOSE ALL GILLIANS ?!
NO!

PRMMMMMMMMMMMMM

GET READY.

WHAM
TOMO
BOOM!!
KRAK
KRAK
KRAK
HERE'S ONE MORE BOOM!

366. The Revenger's High

366. The Revenger's High

SHIRA
SHEEN

FHASH
AAAH !!
RARARAR

BOOM
THWAK
MASHIRO KICK!!

SHINK
YA!
KICK !!
KICK!
KICK!
THOOM

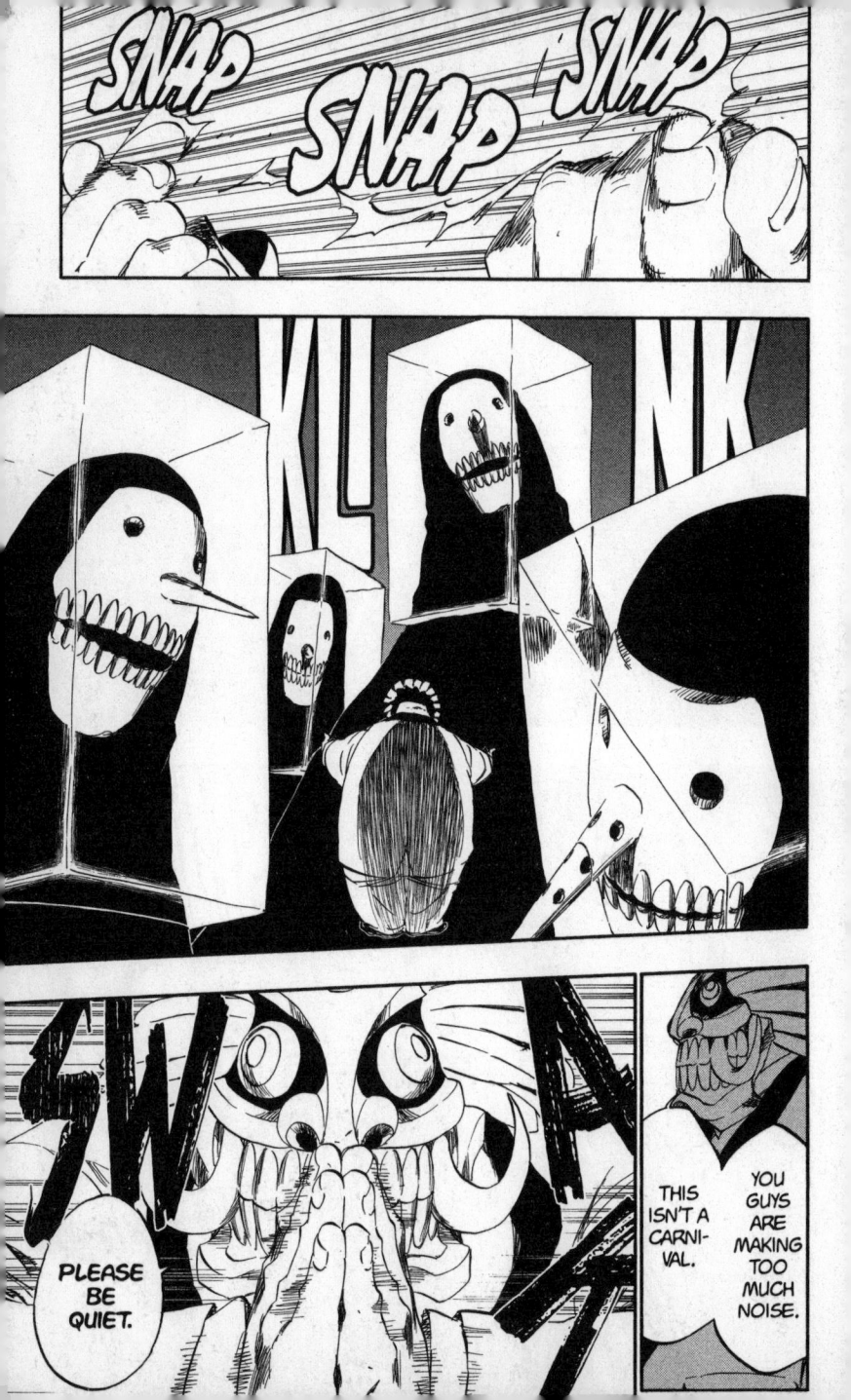
SNAP
SNAP
SNAP
KLANK
YOU GUYS ARE MAKING TOO MUCH NOISE.
THIS ISN'T A CARNI-VAL.
PLEASE BE QUIET.

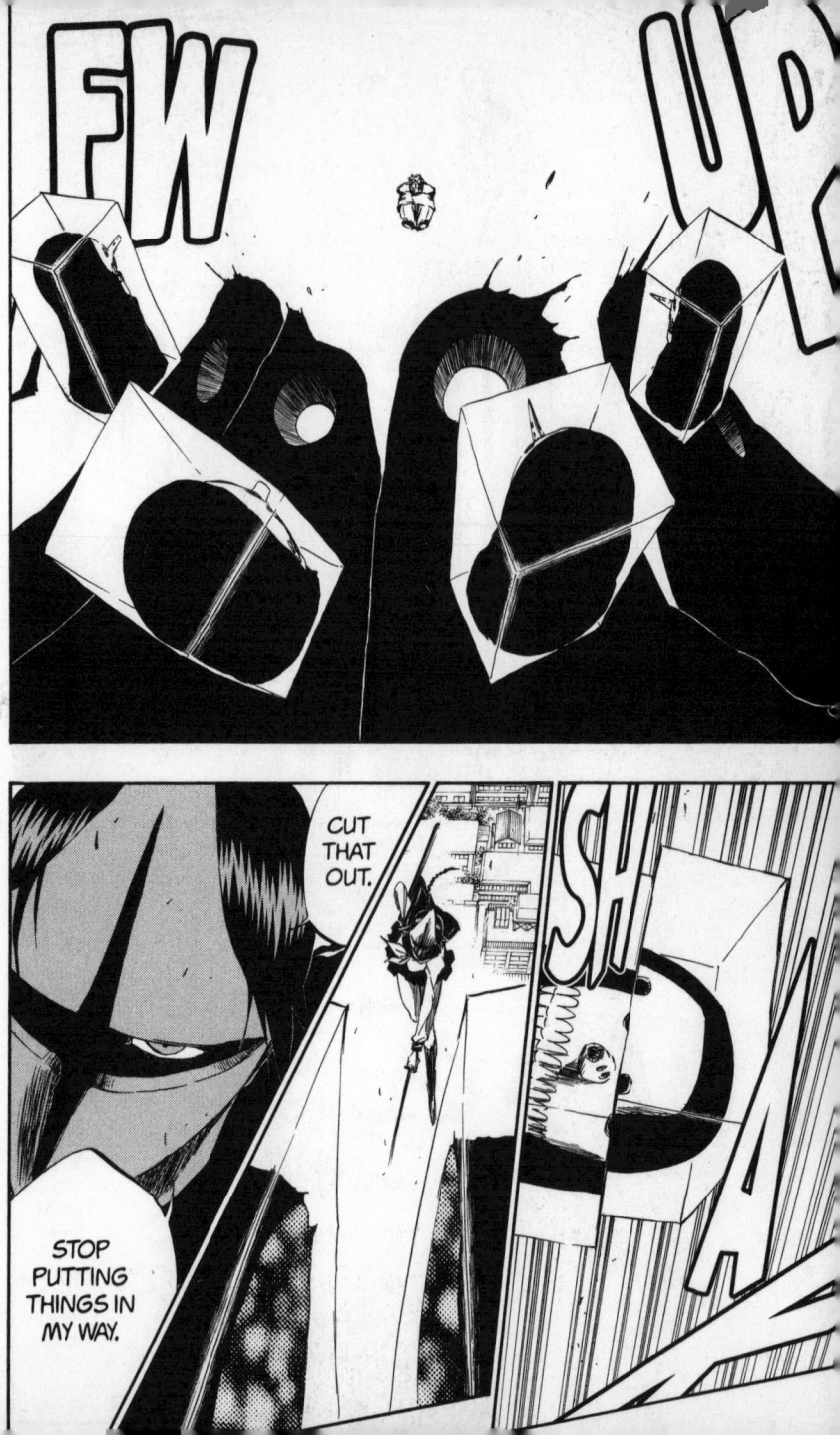
FW
UP
SH
A
CUT THAT OUT.
STOP PUTTING THINGS IN MY WAY.

SWAH
HE EN
TUMP

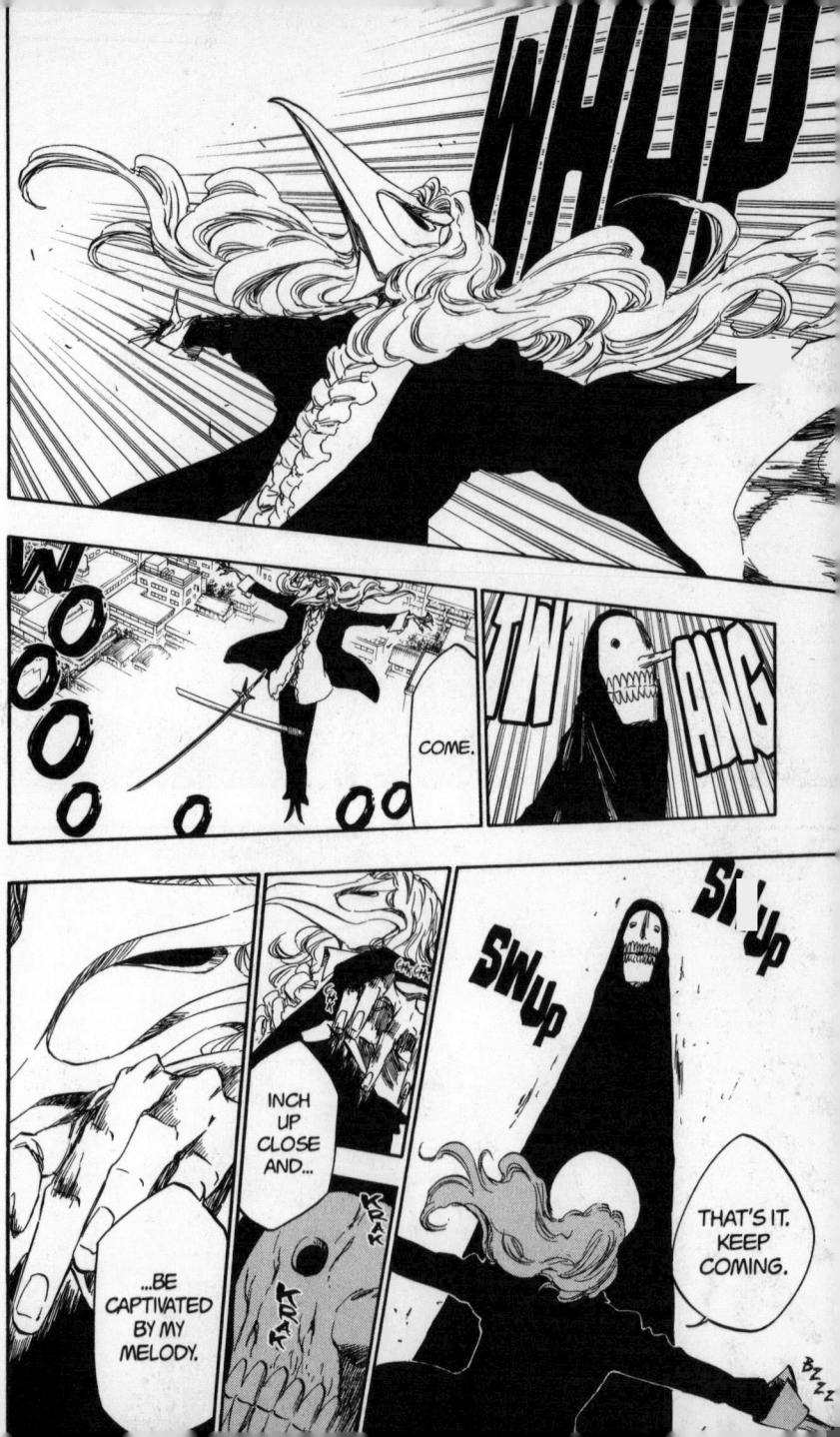
WHUP
WOOOOOO
COME.
TWANG
SWUP
SWUP
THAT'S IT. KEEP COMING.
BZZZ
INCH UP CLOSE AND...
KOAK
...BE CAPTIVATED BY MY MELODY.

SLASH

CLANK

SHRIK
PLOP
WHO

W–
WHOA!!
THEY'RE CRAZY STRONG!!
WHAT... ARE THESE GUYS?!

...AIZEN?

WELL?
WE'VE GOTTEN PRETTY GOOD AT CONTROLLING OUR HOLLOW-FICATION, HAVEN'T WE...

LET'S END THIS.

YOU FELL FOR IT, LOSER.
HEH HEH HEH ...
TORUE, DEPARTMENT CHIEF RESEARCH AND DEVELOPMENT DEPARTMENT RESEARCH MATERIAL CAPTURE DIVISION
THE RESEARCH AND DEVELOPMENT DEPARTMENT HAS FINALLY CAPTURED KON! WHAT WILL THEY DO TO HIM?! FIND OUT IN THE NEXT VOLUME!
TO BE CONT'D

367. YOUR ENEMY IS MY ENEMY

I MISS-ED.
SH RSHI
CHAK

ARE YOU CRAZY ?
YOU GOT ME.
BIG WORDS FOR A FLUNKY ...
TAT
MY INTENTION WAS TO SLICE YOUR HEAD OFF JUST ABOVE YOUR LEFT EYE.
I DON'T COUNT THAT AS A HIT.
FWIK
CHAK
THEN HOW HUMILI-ATING IT MUST BE...
...TO BE KILLED BY A FLUNKY.

KOMA-MURA !!
LET ME HELP YOU...
...MASKED VISITOR.

YOU SURE ...
...YOU WANT TO HELP US ODD-BALLS?
AL-THOUGH ...
FROM THE LOOK OF THINGS, YOU'RE PRETTY ODD YOUR-SELF.
YOU PEOPLE DIDN'T HESITATE TO CONFRONT THE MENOS GRANDES.
THAT IS REASON ENOUGH FOR ME TO HELP YOU!
I'VE DECIDED TO FIGHT AT YOUR SIDE!
I WON'T HEAR ANY OBJEC-TIONS, MASKED VISITOR!
WHAT'S UP WITH THIS GUY?
I'M NOT GOOD AT DEALING WITH STIFF PEOPLE LIKE HIM.

HE SURE MADE HIS INTENTIONS KNOWN.
BUT WE DEFINITELY...
KOMA-MURA!

WHAM
WASH

...DON'T HAVE TIME TO WONDER...
...WHETHER YOU'RE FRIENDS OR ENEMIES.

BLEACH 367.
HMPH!

THAT'S RIGHT.
WE DON'T REALLY WANT TO HELP YOU SOUL REAPERS EITHER!
BUT NOW'S NOT THE TIME TO ARGUE ABOUT THAT!

TMP
IT DOESN'T TAKE MUCH...
...TO TURN STRANGERS INTO COMRADES.

AN ENEMY'S ENEMY IS AN ALLY!
ISN'T THAT REASON ENOUGH?
HMPH.
CLAK

YOUR ENEMY IS MY ENEMY
I CAN'T ARGUE WITH THAT.
BAM

HEY !!
BOOM

SPLP
YOU CAN HAVE THAT BIG ONE OVER THERE, SO STOP WHINING!
SHUT UP!
THE LAST ONE BELONGED TO ME!

...OVER THERE.
THE BIG ONE...

KLONK
A COMMON ENEMY...
...
I LOVE YOU, KENSEI !!
YAY!

KLAK
SOLIDARITY IN THE FACE OF A COMMON ENEMY IS SAID TO BE A HUMAN FAILING.
BUT THAT'S NOT TRUE.

IT'S NOT A FAILING. IT'S A SURVIVAL INSTINCT OF LIVING CREATURES.
WHAP
IN FACT, AT MOMENTS LIKE THESE, EMOTIONAL SOLIDARITY IS AN ASSET.

THE DISCUSSION'S OVER!
STOP YAPPING AND CONCENTRATE ON WHAT'S IN FRONT OF YOU.
WHAT WAS THAT FOR, LOVE ?!
OW!

LOOK.
HE SEEMS STRONG.
IT ONLY LASTS FOR THREE MINUTES.
BECAUSE WE'RE HEROES.
YOU THINK SO?
YOU SURE YOU WANT YOUR MASK OFF?

BWOOO...
PLIP
PLIP
PLIP
HMM ...
MASHI-RO...
RRMM

HWAK
SUPER KICK!!
POP
POP
POP
POP

IT'S THE OPPO-SITE ...
...OF THE TIME BEFORE.

I WOULD NEVER HAVE GUESSED THAT I WOULD HAVE TO BLOCK YOUR SWORD TO PROTECT SOMEBODY.
...
I KNEW.

CHAK
THAT WE WOULD EVEN-TUALLY ...
...FIGHT TO THE DEATH.
WHUP
ARE YOU READY?

CHANK
KILLN
K
TMP
I'M SORRY, CAPTAIN KOMA-MURA.

TMP
LET ME...
...JOIN THIS FIGHT!
PLEASE...
HISAGI!
...

D0037048
CONTI
NUED
IN
BLEACH
43